Preparing to Celebrate with Youth

Marilyn J. Sweet

NOVALIS
THE LITURGICAL PRESS

Design: Eye-to-Eye Design, Toronto

Layout: Suzanne Latourelle

Illustrations: Eugene Kral

Series Editor: Bernadette Gasslein

© 1997, Novalis, Saint Paul University, Ottawa, Ontario, Canada

Business Office: Novalis, 49 Front Street East, 2nd floor, Toronto, ON M5E 1B3

Published in the United States of America by The Liturgical Press, Box 7500, Collegeville, MN 56321-7500.

Novalis ISBN 2 89088 804 5

The Liturgical Press: ISBN 0-8146-2515-0
A Liturgical Press Book.
Library of Congress data available on request.

Printed in Canada

Sweet, Marilyn, J., 1947-
Preparing to celebrate with youth

(Preparing for liturgy)
Includes bibliographical references.
ISBN 2-89088-804-5

1. Youth in public worship. 2. Catholic Church–Liturgy. I. Title. II Series.

BX1970.S84 1997   264L02'00835   C97-900972-3

Contents

Introduction

If you've been worrying about working with young people in liturgy, relax, and give thanks! This is a valuable opportunity to make friends under the best conditions, joining young people in encountering the Risen Lord. You will be renewed while you share your faith in a variety of ways. You can nurture gifts, teach skills, listen attentively, affirm talents and intuitions, encourage creativity and a sense of responsibility, and foster leadership. To do this well you need a willing heart, belief in and respect for young people, the support of your faith community, faith in the God who calls us all to wholeness, love for the church, a strong grip on reality and a good dose of common sense, an appreciation of worship as "the source and the summit of the life of the Christian community" (*Constitution on the Sacred Liturgy* [*CSL*], 10), an understanding of the components of liturgy, and access to the resources necessary to develop a worthy worship experience for all participants.

Young people are the lifeblood of our world, today and tomorrow. They thirst for meaning in their lives. They are capable of "full, conscious and active participation in liturgical celebrations" (*CSL*, 14) that will nourish them. Repeated through the cycle of the seasons, the experience of *good* liturgy will help sustain youth in their difficult periods when nothing seems to mean very much. We must honour youth by providing our very best resources and expecting honest, wholehearted responses.

Those who prepare celebrations with young people are entrusted with the task of guiding and supporting them as they accept their roles in the community. We can be like the scribe in Matthew's gospel who is trained for the kingdom of heaven, bringing out of the treasury things both old and new (Mt 13: 52). Our privilege is to open the treasure chest and expose the many gifts therein, encouraging our young friends to draw nourishment from our common heritage.

In preparing to pray with young people we have two of the best reasons for excellence—God and youth. In liturgy the Holy

Spirit enables us to enter Christ's prayer of thanksgiving to the Father, and we offer our worship to the Almighty God who calls us into life, sustaining and supporting us at every point in the journey of faith. In liturgy we enter actively into the paschal mystery. Nothing shabby, careless or pretentious can be allowed to mar this essential act of life.

This book, *Preparing to Celebrate with Youth*, aims to offer basic information on the principles underlying liturgy planning, the basics required to do this well with young people, and practical points to enable people to prepare with some degree of comfort and skill. I hope this book will raise the standard of excellence for liturgies involving young people, so that all believers can more readily enter into the experience of the paschal mystery. Please use it as a guide, not a straitjacket!

In Summary

1. Young people have much to share with the faith community, and experience deep hunger for meaning. Support them with excellent resources and expect a rich response.

2. Preparing liturgy is an excellent area for work with young believers, helping them to grow in faith and sustaining them in times of crisis. It is a wise and worthwhile investment of time and energy.

Discussion Questions

1. What in your church experience attracts young people?

2. What do you value most at worship? Why? How would you express this to young people who are preparing worship?

3. What is your best memory of participating in liturgy? What factors made it so good?

CHAPTER 1

Real Members, Just as They Are

In the years between twelve and twenty-four, young people experience transformation in every aspect of life. Unpredictable physical changes seem to occur overnight. Often the body does what the mind doesn't want it to do (and vice versa). Psychological, emotional, intellectual and spiritual development is a major task of these years. Young people move from the complete dependence of childhood through withdrawal and rebellion into independence, and towards the healthy interdependence which marks mature adult relationships. Intellectual functioning changes dramatically to accommodate abstraction and analysis. The family may undergo significant alteration, with the birth of more children, the death of grandparents, parental career changes, the departure and/or return of siblings, and moves from one house to another. There may be family breakdown. The faith development task of these years is to grow from a child living a received faith into a believer who questions, analyses and reflects, and moves towards eventual integration. And while all this change is going on within the young person, the outside world continues to shift at a dizzying pace.

The Church: A Companion in Growth and Change

The church is a companion in this time of growth and change. "The church ... believes that the key, the centre and the purpose of the whole of (human) history is to be found in its Lord and Master. She also maintains that beneath all that changes there is much that is unchanging, much that has its ultimate foundation in Christ, who is the same yesterday and today and forever" (*Pastoral Constitution on the Church in the Modern World*, 10). The church has a great deal to give young people, and can benefit enormously from their challenges, their honesty, and their searching faith. In their seasons of transition, the church can offer youth:

- support and acceptance in the parish community;
- the stories of God's constant care in times of transition as found in scripture, the lives of the saints, and our own lives;
- sacramental celebrations of God's presence in our lives;
- care, in the name of Jesus, for those in need;
- respect for human life at all stages and in all forms;
- honest confession of faults and trust in God's reconciling love;
- commitment to truth and justice;
- witness to integrity.

As we gather Sunday after Sunday, we testify to the constancy of the One in whom we believe. Calling young people to their rightful place in the community of faith encourages them to value their baptismal character as an essential expression of their identity.

Young people can be well nourished by their participation in the church's liturgy. The power of the scriptures and the sacraments, the traditional rituals, the commitment of the faithful to the life of the community, and the breadth and depth of the faith tradition offer a unique frame of reference and valuable support for those searching for deeper meaning. Rock concerts do not take the place of worship, nor does walking in the woods or playing hockey, but all of these experiences will be enriched by the prayer of the community of faith.

Be Realistic

When preparing liturgies with youth, recognize and factor in the adolescent stages of emotional and intellectual growth and faith development, as well as the demands of family life, school and sports. Preparing a rich celebration of evening prayer as a beginning to the school year is a wonderful idea. Scheduling it at the same time as the soccer tournament and expecting the goal keeper to be the reader is a prescription for disappointment and conflict. Using music and prayers developed for those in the early elementary grades insults young people in junior high who will not be willing to return to another such liturgy. Dull words delivered in a monotone by a presider who avoids eye contact with the assembly leads to a verdict of 'boring.' Young people instinctively know that liturgy is the work of the whole assembled community and seek to take part in meaningful ways.

In Summary

1. Intense, rapid, radical change, which can cause turbulence and confusion, characterizes this stage of life.

2. The church can offer youth meaningful companionship, support and stability.

3. Young people, as baptized members of the assembly, have a rightful place in the church. In their absence the whole community is diminished.

4. In working with young people, be aware of the many demands on their time and spirit. Offer companionship, not competition.

Discussion Questions

1. What is the right place for young people in your parish? How is this expressed?

2. How is your participation in liturgy an act of love? How do you share that love with young people whose worship experience has not been positive?

3. How do you continue to welcome and accept teenagers who are not taking part in the Sunday assembly at this time?

CHAPTER 2

Beware of These Traps!

Avoid these pitfalls when preparing to celebrate with youth. Some commonly accepted statements about liturgy and young people are simply not true.

Don't Imitate Music Videos or Movies

Church and entertainment are totally different worlds, and young people relate differently to each. Teenagers are the object of the music industry. Believers are the subject of the act of worship, joining with Christ in praising God. There is no audience in church. Any attempt to develop liturgies that imitate music videos or copy movies will fail as worship *and* as entertainment.

Novelty Is Not Always Better

Rituals and traditions do provide reliable landmarks in a turbulent life. Novelty is not always better, or more attractive to young people. It is good to begin our prayer together "in the name of the Father and of the Son and of the Holy Spirit." We remember again who we are, and join each other on the familiar path of our common prayer. In our rituals and prayer traditions, we express our shared experience and identity. We reach into our past to understand and express our present experience and to name our hopes for the future. Ritual helps us to know ourselves as part of the community of faith. A clear directive in the *Directory for Masses with Children* (21), which provides that nothing is to be done in liturgies with children that will prevent their joining in worship with the larger community at the Sunday asssembly, is equally useful at this age. This provision protects the shared ritual experience which is so important to the individual and to the community.

Balance the Familiar and the Innovative

Young people are formed in the practices of our faith when they share in the community's common prayer, but that does not mean everything must always be done exactly the same way. Liturgy that honestly expresses the lives of the participants will certainly be influenced by cultural practices. The old established ways are not the only ways, and they can blend very well with new expressions. Learn which elements can be adapted and which must be retained in a specific form. A healthy balance between the familiar and the innovative will form the community in the habit of prayer, and stimulate it to be alert to the unexpected action of God in its life.

Liturgy Is Liturgy

Liturgy is a communal experience of ritual worship, an act of love. It is neither catechetics, nor a civic ceremony. It is not something done *by* some leaders to some followers. It is not the time to teach morality and doctrine, lecture about behaviour, campaign for a particular point of view, or praise people's achievements. It is the moment to enter most completely into the paschal mystery, sharing in Jesus Christ's praise of God who blesses us with the gifts of life and love.

Liturgy is Prayer, Not Performance

Because it is a formal public activity, and the actions of several people do intersect, preparation and rehearsal are necessary, but liturgy is not performance or drama. This is the authentic activity of people expressing the reality of their lives. In the preface dialogue, "Let us give thanks to the Lord our God. / It is right to give God thanks and praise," the community is really agreeing to move forward into the great eucharistic prayer of thanksgiving. The lector's voice actually speaks "the word of the Lord." The communion minister's ritual phrase, "the body of Christ," points to the reality that, in serving small pieces of bread to classmates, he or she is truly serving the body of Christ to the body of Christ.

Liturgy: Aways Authentic and Excellent

Liturgy need not be elaborate, but it should always be authentic and excellent. A grimy or cluttered worship space, a mumbled reading of scripture, a tedious or smug homily, a hunk of soggy bread, or an over-abundance of extra events within the liturgy all interfere with the prayer of the community. Plastic flowers, taped songs, 'creative' scripture translations, 'spontaneous' additions or changes to the eucharistic prayer all introduce discordant notes of artificiality and individualism that impede authentic participation in Christ's prayer to the Father and interfere with the formation of the Christian community.

Liturgy Can't Stand Alone

Liturgy can't carry the full weight of forming young people in faith, and it can't stand alone. The *Constitution on the Sacred Liturgy* advises "… it is necessary that the faithful come to it with proper dispositions, that their minds be attuned to their voices, and that they cooperate with divine grace ..." (*CSL*, 11). Young people must be called to faith and conversion. They need education in faith, guidance and formation in personal prayer, and the encouragement of the Christian community. We must challenge them to lead lives that proclaim the good news of Christ. That work must be done by those who share in the community life of prayer, and it must be informed by the common experience of worship.

Many discussions about young people's noticeable lack of enthusiasm for church lead to attempts to "jazz up the mass" or "take out the boring parts." This doomed effort to fix the symptom neglects such basic causes as the stages of adolescent development, the selfishness fostered by this society's consumerism and individualism, a profound mistrust of ordained leaders, and a lack of fundamental faith formation.

The adolescent's developmental need to act independently can conflict with the family's expectation that everyone will share in Sunday mass together. Assisting all family members to appreciate the extensive and conflicting variety of needs within the family, and facilitating some basic negotiations that lead to respectful conflict resolution is an important contribution to evangelisation and the growth of the worshipping community.

The church is called to be counter-cultural in the face of those contemporary attitudes that destroy life and the community of love which reflects God's love. Attempts to imitate the entertainment industry or follow the dictates of the fashion world make a lie of the worship experience and rob young people of the voice of the gospel. Antidotes to the illnesses of today's world are found in the stories from scripture, but the connections must be made clear. The story of Jesus healing Jairus' daughter (Mark 5:22-24, 35-43) is just another miracle story until we make the point that, to care for her, Jesus had to break every societal norm. The testimonies and martyrdoms recorded in the Acts of the Apostles are just ancient history until we ask the question, "What do I consider important enough to die for? What are the values that I show every day by the way I live my life?" This kind of reflection, which demands a generous expenditure of time and respectful listening, is an investment that bears rich fruit in discipleship, and brings new life to the liturgy.

The revelations of sexual abuse perpetrated by some members of the clergy on some young people have led to a profound disruption in the relationships between clergy and youth in general. Many young people today begin from a position of "no trust and little respect" for the ordained leadership of the church. There are clerics whose relationships with young people are infected with a profound fear of suspicion and lawsuit. Such an atmosphere certainly impedes the liturgical celebration, and it will not be eased by better music or a new prayer. What may help, however, is open, honest discussion about failure, sin and grace, about the demands of leadership and the reality of the Christian community, and about the risks of faithful living. It is also important that young people and those ministering with them receive pertinent information about the signs of and contributing factors to abuse, as well as basic instruction in self-protection.

Young people whose faith has not been formed in our common story will find it difficult to be full, conscious and active participants in the liturgical practice and ritual language rooted in our faith tradition. They lack the frame of reference and conceptual tools to enter it with any depth. Lectionary-based faith development programming will make a tremendous difference.

I list these common concerns, not to discourage, but because good solid information is one of our very best tools for addressing the challenges of this work. Understanding the scope of the issues is as important as knowing how to select readings.

Young people participate more effective when they are actively involved in preparation and ministry. While taking part in the planning and preparation, they will be developing their faith in a variety of healthy ways. At its best, working with young people can be a positive experience of mentoring, as you share your resources and your knowledge, while learning from them. You can trust young people to meet their commitments, and expect them to put time in for preparation and practice when they understand why it is important. They can assume responsibility for peer ministry. Participation in liturgy cannot be imposed on anyone, but shared leadership will encourage more young people to take an active role in the prayer of their own group, and in the prayer of the Sunday assembly. It is worth the effort, bears valuable fruit, and enacts a very good model of church.

In Summary

1. Liturgy, an act of love and shared ritual, is the work of all present.

2. Sunday mass cannot offer all the formation for Christians of any age. Deliberate action by members of the faith community encourages the ongoing conversion of youth.

3. Be prepared to acknowledge and discuss honestly the many obstacles to young people's participation in church life.

Discussion Questions

1. How does faith formation help young people contribute more to the liturgy?

2. What are the obvious, and not-so-obvious signs of "people as audience" liturgy?

3. What can young people do if they determine the Sunday liturgy in their own parish is generally boring?

CHAPTER 3

Full, Conscious and Active Participation

A familiar scene is the row of young people sitting at the back of the church, waiting until they can leave. Their arms are crossed, bodies slouched, faces set in stone because someone has just told them to stop their talking. Yet they have come. Their presence challenges the whole community to help them know they are important to the celebration.

Consider the value the church places on such participation:

> The church, therefore, earnestly desires that Christ's faithful, when present at this mystery of faith, should not be there as strangers or silent spectators. On the contrary, through a good understanding of the rites and prayers, they should take part in the sacred action, conscious of what they are doing, with devotion and full collaboration. They should be instructed by God's word, and be nourished at the table of the Lord's body. They should give thanks to God. Offering the immaculate victim not only through the hands of the priest, but also together with him, they should learn to offer themselves. Through Christ, the Mediator, they should be drawn day by day into ever more perfect union with God and with each other, so that finally God may be all in all (CSL, 48).

The Sunday assembly can express each person's importance to the community of faith in a variety of ways, beginning with the first act of the Christian assembly, hospitality. Ministers of hospitality speak *for* all of us, and *to* all of us, as they ensure there is room to park, adequate access to the church and suitable seating, distribute helpful participation aids, and greet people warmly. Young people feel this hospitality when they are greeted by name and accepted no matter what they may be wearing, when some of their peers share in the ministry of hospitality, when there is a place for them to sit, when they are treated as young adults instead of grade-school children, and when they experience the liturgy as speaking in some way to their experience. The Sunday assembly is for all members of the household of God.

Adolescence is a time of change, a period of developing a specific identity distinct from the family. It is an opportunity to try out new and different things, and to break out of established patterns and rituals. During this time youth need a safe harbour, where everything is familiar and secure, when change has become too great and transitions too demanding. When young people can express themselves at church just by choosing another seat, or another mass time, when we encourage them to try out a new ministry or help select new music, when we invite them back after they have been away for a while, when they can accept responsibilities and meet new people, when the music, prayers and preaching touch their lives, they discover they can still find a place to belong in the church.

Inviting youth to take part in particular ministries can help build their sense of belonging to and responsibility for the worship life of the community. As we encourage young people to take a ministerial role, and instruct and assist them so that they can meet the expectations that come with ministry, other young people begin to see and believe that the church needs and wants them to be part of the celebration. And as young people begin to accept their responsibilities as maturing members of the community of faith, fulfilling duties as scheduled and supporting the parish with their presence, adult members of the parish begin to trust and welcome them as partners in ministry. All of this nurtures their sense of being valued as individual members of the community.

Importance of Reflection

One of the great challenges in liturgy preparation is to enable the assembly to accept its role as liturgical minister. The individualism and consumerism which mark this age affect our worship to the point where an acceptable reason for skipping mass is "I don't get anything out of it." The patterned response "Well, have you put anything into it?" only continues the attitude. The reality is that liturgy is the life and work of the church and we, together with other baptized persons, form the church. At times our emotional experience will be minimal, but worship is far deeper than our personal feelings on a particular day. It is a lifelong commitment, and we become involved participants through regular practice and an attitude of the heart.

Reflecting on the demands and influence of liturgical ministry on life is crucial. Encourage young people to live their Christian commitment faithfully. Continue to support them with friendship and acceptance when the events of their lives impel them to stay away from worship, or withdraw from liturgical ministry.

You don't need to do anything exotic or different to entice young people to become active participants in our faith communities. Be hospitable, accepting, supportive; make room, have high expectations. Be prepared for change. Present the ancient valued truths of our faith. Prepare good liturgies with competent ministries, preach well, proclaim the gospel, tell the truth. Work to make the hospitality and witness of Sunday morning authentic the rest of the week, for young people, like the rest of us, are entitled to support as they come to terms with difficult life questions. Accept that the emotional and spiritual fluctuations in young people's lives will be expressed in their church participation. And, most importantly, realize that if young people are an active and valued part of the parish, there will be challenges—and energy and activity. If your community does not welcome, treasure and express that energy in its worship, then young people will withdraw.

Common Gestures and Postures

Full, conscious and active participation is more easily experienced when all share in common gestures and postures, such as making the sign of the cross, eagerly standing at the first sound of the gospel Alleluia, extending hands in response to the presider's gestures of welcome, standing to express belief and commitment, stretching arms wide to pray the Lord's Prayer, greeting those nearby with a sign of peace. Planners and presiders can help young people share in and appreciate the importance of these gestures and postures. After the liturgy, group reflection on the meaning of specific gestures and the feelings associated with the experience can help strengthen the experience, and reinforce the practice. Education about gesture and posture will stay with young people as they continue to participate in the community's prayer.

Processions

Good processions express the unity of the assembly, and call all into shared ministry; they create energy and excitement. People can join in the entrance procession on special occasions, circling the entire assembly area before moving to their places. They could carry palm branches on Palm Sunday, tapers at Easter, wildflowers in summer, and sheaves of oats at Thanksgiving.

We must recognize, however, that in our most common and most important procession of all, the communion procession, many people behave as if they were all alone in the world with Jesus. This is a fertile spot for presiders, planners and musicians to work for change. Encourage young people to move away from private piety and come forward, singing joyfully, in harmony with all in the assembly, to feast at the Lord's table.

To develop good processions:

- Select music with a good rhythm that encourages people to move and with simple refrains that people can sing;
- Determine a simple path, remove all obstacles, and prepare leaders who will move forward with confidence;
- When appropriate, arrange for flowers, banners, tapers, or other material to be carried.

Watch for opportunities to have processions, prepare well, and join in enthusiastically.

In Summary

1. Genuine hospitality is the first and most basic liturgical act.

2. Serving in liturgical ministry helps young people experience their baptismal belonging to the Christian community and energizes and challenges the whole community.

3. Meaningful ritual actions foster authentic participation.

Discussion Questions

1. What can ministers of hospitality do to welcome young people?

2. What meaningful gestures will a liturgical gathering of young people willingly share in?

3. What does the communion procession at your parish Sunday mass look like? Is there a great difference between that procession and the one at the mass with all the young people?

CHAPTER 4

Preparation

Immediate and long-term preparation for liturgy are two very important, interrelated activities that help the community pray well. Every liturgical celebration requires some immediate preparation. There are vessels to fill, linens to lay out, books to be set, and a multitude of other tasks both large and small. The well-prepared musician will have all the music properly arranged, so that pages do not fall out and there is no need to rustle all the papers during the liturgy of the word. The provident sacristan will have a list of what should be on the credence table. And the presider will check the setting of the sacramentary so he does not convey the impression he does not know what should be happening. There is no substitute for careful preparation of all the details.

There is long-range preparation, too, in which young people can share. The group could include individuals who will serve as presider, musician, hospitality minister, sacristan, preparer of the environment, and lector. It is important that the cares and concerns, as well as the hopes and dreams of the community which will be celebrating together, be expressed at preparation sessions. It is equally important that the group work from a fundamental appreciation of liturgical principles. As we start to prepare the community's prayer, we don't start from scratch, but draw from the church's scriptures and rituals. (For more on this process, see *Preparing and Evaluating Liturgy* in this series.)

Reflection together after the liturgy is the other essential element that completes the preparation process. Planners need to ask questions about their own and others' experience of the celebration to develop some sense of what drew the community into common prayer and what got in the way.

Needs and possibilities differ greatly according to circumstances: Liturgy with a group that meets once a year for a three-day youth festival is very different from a Sunday celebration in the parish or weekday mass in the high school gym.

Extensive advance preparation can take place when you know a community will gather at specified times. The preparation team in a Catholic high school, for example, can determine which liturgies will be celebrated when, and can also arrange for ongoing liturgical and theological formation to assist the community's prayer. They can outline preparation requirements, train ministers, procure objects to enhance the environment, develop a program for introducing music to the community, and explore the potential of the liturgical seasons.

Unity and Balance

"The power of a liturgical celebration to share faith will frequently depend upon its unity—a unity drawn from the liturgical feast or season or from the readings appointed in the lectionary, as well as artistic unity flowing from the skillful and sensitive selection of options, music and related arts" (*Music in Catholic Worship*, 11). Unity and balance in a particular liturgy depend upon a number of factors, many of which can be addressed in the preparation process. Some cannot be anticipated, and will require careful adaptation on the part of the presider, musicians and other ministers.

Unity and balance are interrelated. Balance is a matter of proportion. It is affected by many factors, including the length and complexity of elements, the quality and type of language, music and art, the relative importance of each liturgical unit, the duration and quality of the silences built into the liturgy, the order and placement of elements within the celebration, and the relationships among the ministers and with the entire assembly.

The unity of the celebration draws attention to its focus and predominant theme: the paschal mystery. All liturgy is most profoundly Christ's act of thanksgiving: the unity of the celebration stems from these fundamental realities. Too many secondary factors cloud the central action and distract worshippers. Careful attention to the relationship between the core elements and the secondary factors protects the integrity of the celebration.

Some examples will help to illustrate these points:

- In any eucharistic celebration, the proclamation of scripture, the eucharistic prayer and the communion of the assembly are the central elements. An entrance rite with an extensive personal examination of conscience, a prolonged confession of sinfulness and a ritual gesture of contrition made before the altar by each member of the community, followed by a long drama after the gospel, would disturb the balance of the central elements.
- In morning and evening prayer, the gospel is proclaimed in the singing of the canticle: the *Benedictus* in the morning and the *Magnificat* in the evening. If the reading chosen is also a gospel, the balance is upset.
- The liturgy of the hours is dedicated to psalm-singing and intercessory prayer. If a homilist preaches for forty-five minutes, the focus shifts so much that the unity is marred.

The use of videos, slides or tapes is a technological influence that intrudes on the common action of the assembly. Such material, mistakenly, is used more often in celebrations with young people to entice them to participate or because someone thinks "they will feel more at home if this technology is used." Worshippers, however, are the subject of the liturgical action, not its object, and worship is not entertainment.

In liturgies with young people, music frequently throws the whole celebration off balance. It may be too loud, there may be too many instruments, the pieces may be too long or the selections may not suit the other elements of the liturgy. If the musicians and the presider are constantly trying to outdo each other, the unity of the celebration is destroyed. Music in worship is about serving the liturgy, not about giving a concert. A sense of balance is absolutely essential to musical leadership.

The periods of silence in the liturgy are very important to the balance and unity of the event. Musicians who always fill every moment of silence, or presiders who eliminate the pauses after the invitations to prayer disturb the balance that is built into the liturgy. Allowing time for silence is one of the best ways to express the prayer of the entire community. Rushing along implies that only particular ministers play an active role in this liturgy.

Keeping the liturgical units in appropriate order is important. This importance becomes obvious in a liturgy of the word
in which a "few extra things" are being incorporated. Add other
elements carefully, paying attention to the movement of the
liturgical action, the ritual order and the integrity of prayer
units. For example, ministers are installed and symbols given in
response to hearing the word of God; therefore, such a ritual
properly takes place after the scriptures have been proclaimed
and broken open by the homilist. To install a new youth leader
in an entrance rite does not express the response to God's word
which brings a person to ministry.

The use of appropriate symbols affects liturgy in various
ways. Our primary symbols engage our senses in the reality of our sacraments: gathered community, fresh water, fra-
grant oil, broken bread, rich wine, healing touch, candle
light, spoken word, embrace of peace. The use of other symbols must be proportionate and appropriate. For example,
the church's symbols of new life that express the resur-
rection are baptismal water and the paschal candle;
they speak of dying and rising, and should not be
displaced by butterflies and crystal prisms, which
do not.

Choosing the Form of Liturgy

On Sunday and the great feasts such as the Easter Triduum and
Christmas, the entire parish community celebrates together.
These events express the rich variety of the household of God,
where believers of all ages and stages share in the common celebration of God's love. As full members of this community
through the sacraments of baptism, confirmation and eucharist,
teenagers sharing in their parish worship offer a valuable witness to the action of God in their lives.

There are many other opportunities for young people to
gather for worship in smaller, more homogeneous groups.
Remember, however, that, although the preparation for a particular celebration may focus on the needs of a specific group,
liturgy always belongs to the whole community of faith, and no
one should be excluded or experience a lack of hospitality.

In preparing for prayer, choose from one of the three basic liturgical types: liturgy of the word, liturgy of the hours, or eucharist. Then develop the layers of liturgical elements that will shape and give texture to this specific worship event. The day and time, the circumstances and expectations of the celebrating community, and the availability of ministers determine the choice of liturgy.

The most familiar liturgy, the heart of Christian life, is the celebration of eucharist, the mass. The liturgy of the word, also called a bible service, is the simplest liturgical celebration. The liturgy of the hours, which includes both morning and evening prayer, is the daily prayer of the church.

Eucharist

The parish Sunday eucharist is clearly central to the life of the Christian community and should not be overtaken by any other event. During the week, the community may celebrate eucharist or a liturgy of the word at any hour, but eucharist is not to be repeated on the same day with the same group.

Liturgy of the hours

Morning prayer may be celebrated any time from early in the morning until mid-morning, and evening prayer from late in the afternoon until mid-evening. It does not make much sense to celebrate morning prayer at noon or evening prayer at midnight: a liturgy of the word or night prayer is more appropriate to these times. Liturgy of the hours is best when there is good musical leadership in the community, and some members of the group are accustomed to praying together. Formal evening prayer, enriched by generous symbols and a great deal of singing, may be just the right liturgy for celebrating important community events like graduation.

The simple liturgy of the word format is easily adapted to different times and settings. A liturgy of the word can be short and simple, serving as the opening and/or closing prayer for an active day. It can also be more elaborate, incorporating other liturgical elements, or it can be the setting for a major preaching event. Distribution of holy communion belongs within the celebration of eucharist and should not be included in a liturgy of the word or hours, except on Sunday when the bishop has made provision for it to take place in a community where there is no priest to preside at the eucharist.

To decide what form the liturgy will take, you might ask:

- What is the liturgical event? The season? What does the liturgical season call us to? The liturgies for the Easter Triduum are prescribed, for example, but there are few specifications for a simple weekday in July.
- What is happening in the community, and in the lives of the young people who will participate? Is it graduation week, or have people come together for the first time?
- What liturgical ministers are available and what liturgy will best allow participation? Don't plan eucharist if there is no priest, and do make sure you have a cantor for sung evening prayer. If your group loves to sing and frequently prays the psalms, choose liturgy of the hours.
- What is the nature of the group? Does it meet every week for prayer and discussion of social justice issues, or is it a collection of individuals gathering to pray for a friend who has been missing for a week?
- How much time is there? Do people expect to pray for a very brief moment and then move on to a meeting, or is this the middle of a weekend retreat devoted to listening to God's voice?

The various ritual books provide for the sacraments and prayers of the church. All sacraments are celebrations of the faith community. It is most appropriate that the sacraments of initiation take place within the Sunday assembly, since the Sunday assembly is the heart of the community which welcomes new members. The sacraments of reconciliation and anointing of the sick, however, might well take place within the specific context of a gathering of young people, and so the readings, preaching, prayers, gestures and music could be fitted to that particular assembly. Expressive ritual gestures can be very helpful and are most appropriate to these sacramental celebrations. The prayer language, readings and preaching for a celebration of the sacrament of the sick in a senior citizens' home should sound very different from that for a gathering of senior high students recovering from injuries received on a school bus trip.

The celebrations of the stages in the funeral rite can be adapted to the needs of young people, and should be. The *Order of Christian Funerals* provides a section for the Funeral Rites for Children, and offers adaptations at various points for the funeral of a young person. In the funeral rites, as in all the prayers of the church, it is important to make selections that will console and encourage young people with the support of our faith in language and gesture that are accessible to them.

Non-liturgical prayer

Other forms of prayer would not strictly be considered liturgy. Meditation, listening to taped music, quiet reflection on objects from nature or art, scripture-sharing, hymn sings, and other forms of prayer are very good experiences for young people and serve to lead them to an experience of God within their own daily lives. In a meditative prayer time, for example, the community might sit quietly to hear the gospel. In scripture-sharing, the word of God could be proclaimed without the customary introduction and acclamations. Praying the rosary and the stations of the cross are time-honoured traditional devotions with their own rituals.

Liturgical Seasons

The church celebrates according to its own calendar based on the significant events in the history of salvation. The *General Norms for the Liturgical Year and the Calendar* give extensive information on the factors affecting the calendar. In preparing to celebrate with youth, respect the calendar which expresses the church's liturgical cycle. This will enable young people to enter more fully into the common life of the Christian community, which focuses on the paschal mystery, and those events and persons which reveal that mystery to us.

The temptation to ignore the calendar of the church and focus exclusively on the experience of the youth group can deprive the group of living in the tempo of the paschal mystery. It can separate the young people from the rich life of the Christian community and lead to individualistic expressions of worship.

The challenge to liturgical ministers, especially musicians, homilists and those preparing liturgy, is to connect the lives of worshippers and the life of Christ as expressed in the liturgical year in a way that supports and encourages worshippers to follow Christ in daily life. Each liturgical season provides many points of contact with the lives of young people. (For more on the liturgical year, see *Preparing the Liturgical Year 1* and *Preparing the Liturgical Year 2* in this series.)

Liturgical Books

In preparing liturgies with young people, there is no need to make up anything. The liturgical books of the Canadian church are the best resources available. Most essential are the *Liturgical Calendar*, the *Lectionaries for Sundays and Solemnities* and *for Weekdays*, the *Sacramentary*, and *Catholic Book of Worship III*. A new publication which offers valuable material is *Sunday Celebration of the Word and Hours*. These books provide helpful introductions, explanations of fundamental principles, and all the basics necessary to prepare good celebrations.

Certain common features of these books will help in determining where, when and how adaptations may be made. The introduction to each section of the book explains the reason for the particular rite, and the specific requirements of that time of prayer. An outline of the rite is provided in each setting, listing the elements and their order. Within the rite itself, the rubrics state who—including the assembly—does what. When the prayers may be adapted, the rubric indicates "in these or similar words." Becoming aware of these features will help you develop adaptations most fitting to the liturgy.

Access to these ritual books is important for liturgical planners. Preparing liturgies with youth is just as important as preparing any other liturgy; denying access to these ritual books and other parish resources can impede the participation of young people in the life of the church, and lead to the development of inappropriate, individualistic prayer forms.

The various conferences of bishops have also provided ritual books for the celebration of the sacraments. Familiarity with the introductions which provide the basic principles and the fundamental order of service will make it possible to adapt and adjust as circumstances require. Those preparing liturgies should use the books for their own country (Canadian books in Canada, American in the United States, etc.).

Setting the Space

What does the worship space look like? How do we set up the space so that we can meet the demands of the liturgy and the young people who will gather to pray as a community? Take the time in the worship planning group to think about the space and put some energy into preparing it for worship. Choose the best possible location for the group that will meet, and help the young people feel at home there. A tour of the church can really make a difference in appreciating and understanding the elements and the surroundings that support our prayer. As a general rule, the church, the Christian community's home for prayer, is the best place for worship. Far too often, the youth of the parish are confined to the basement and the parish worship space is virtually off limits to them.

Size

There may, however, be very good reasons for choosing another location. The size of the group will indicate the size of the space. Don't expect ten people to achieve any level of comfort in a marble cathedral that seats a thousand. Twenty-five people squeezed into a prayer space designed to offer a contemplation corner for two or three people cannot come to any kind of prayer except a whispered plea for escape. Adequate lighting and fresh air are essential, and the space must be accessible to all who wish to participate. If the available area is far too large, define a smaller space with your furnishings or plants, or take advantage of an architectural feature that provides some intimacy. If the space is far too small, remove furniture, give thanks for the blessings of an abundant community, and try to find a more suitable space before the group meets again.

Cleanliness

Cleanliness matters. Dust and dirt, cobwebs and discarded tissues all state that this is not a very important activity and can be treated in a shoddy and careless fashion. Take the time to clean up the space ... remove the trash, dispose of the scummy green water, sweep.

Lighting and movement

Those elements necessary for community participation, such as adequate lighting and suitable sound equipment, must be carefully selected and properly placed to serve the community's prayer. The ability to move about easily, and to be seen and heard clearly are also important factors to consider.

In determining the placement of furnishings, remember that in seeing each other's faces, we look on the body of Christ. The seating for the presider and other ministers expresses their relationship to the community. If seating is flexible, resist the temptation to set up the space in row-by-row 'church style' seating. Try a semi-circle instead, or choir formation.

Objects and furnishings

Objects and furnishings which support the prayer of the assembly may include the font and blessed water, the altar, the ambo, seating for the presider and the assembly, the processional cross, the Lectionary and the Book of the Gospels, the paschal candle and other candles, the plate and the cup, the burning incense, the holy oils. A simple standard for selecting liturgical items and furnishing the space for worship is to use the very best that you have available, and use only what is necessary. In choosing furnishings, refuse anything shabby. A solid wood straight chair is a better seat for the presider than a deluxe armchair with ragged upholstery. Dirty and ripped vestments, stubby bits of candle, wilted flowers, soiled linen, tattered books are all unfaithful to the work we do.

Clutter is distracting to worship. Remove extra furnishings if they are moveable and unnecessary. A multitude of crosses or liturgical symbols on vestments and banners, excessive fabric draping and lace trim on every table, great quantities of plants and flowers, or banners with lots of words on them all get in the way of the community's prayer. Return the worship space to its previous state when you are finished.

Young people do appreciate quality and beauty. Preparing the worship space well reflects the importance of the liturgical event and the community that gathers to celebrate.

In Summary

1. Preparation before and reflection after celebration are essential.

2. Attend to unity and balance, and honour the demands of authenticity, quality, timing and order.

3. In preparing, consider the ritual books, the liturgical calendar, the needs of the community, gifts of the assembly, and time and space available.

Discussion Questions

1. How can you include young people in liturgy preparation? How do they begin?

2. Have you browsed through any of the ritual books and located the adaptations possible to meet the needs of young people?

3. What does your worship space say about your community? Is the space accessible to the youth group? How would you adapt it for their needs?

CHAPTER 5

Essentials

Ministers

Liturgy is the work of the people of God gathered in one place. Many services, or ministries, support the prayer of the community. All aspects of that work are to be carried out by members of the community who participate in the entire liturgy.

The basic criteria for all liturgical ministers are initiation, an orientation to the prayer of the community, the skill or talent required to serve the community's need, a commitment to improve with practice and guidance, and respect for the community. All of these prerequisites can be met by competent young people, members of the community with the gifts to serve in a variety of ways. (Full initiation into the Roman Catholic Church includes being baptized and confirmed, and receiving the body and blood of the Lord. Those who are baptized, but have not yet been confirmed or received first communion, are members of the church but are not yet fully initiated.) Certain ministries are reserved to the ordained, specifically, presiding at the celebration of the eucharist, the sacrament of reconciliation, and the anointing of the sick. These cannot be delegated to lay people.

Lay people serve in the variety of liturgical ministries which support the prayer of the assembly, according to their ability. The first minister is the assembly itself. (For more on this topic, see *Preparing the Assembly to Celebrate* in this series.) Group reflection on the liturgical experience will enable young people to become more effective ministers.

A number of specific roles must be carried out for the good order of the community and its prayer. Certain ministers do their work before the celebration begins. Others serve throughout the celebration. A few ministers, such as the lector and the communion minister, perform a particular service at a specified point in the liturgy. The advice in the *General Instruction of the Roman Missal* (58) makes it very clear: "All, whether ministers or laypersons, should do all and only those parts that belong to them, so that the very arrangement of the celebration itself makes the church stand out as being formed in a structure of different orders and ministries."

It is a real challenge to prepare liturgy that will engage young people. It helps to appreciate the importance of the diversity of roles, the balance which must be struck among them, and the fundamental importance of the assembly as minister of the community's prayer. It is wrong to prepare young people for specific ministries in a way which implies that being a reader or a musician is somehow better than "just sitting in the pew."

Performance and display are hostile to ministry, and will pollute the liturgy. Training ministers so that they know their roles and can carry them out well in a true spirit of prayer and service is an effective way to improve the liturgy so that all can participate more effectively.

A word about liturgical vestments. The alb, which represents our baptismal garment, is the full-length white vestment worn by liturgical ministers who preside or serve at mass, the liturgy of the hours or a liturgy of the word. Vestments, a sign of service to the community of the baptized, are to be clean and well-kept, and are to be worn with dignity, respect and humility.

Proclaiming Scripture

Being nourished at the table of God's word is absolutely essential to living the Christian life. Young people will be sustained in their faith by hearing the word of God proclaimed in ways that enable them to receive it as a light to their path.

Effective proclamation of the Scripture in the community of faith demands attention to these basic aspects:

• Select appropriate scripture passages;
• Use the best materials available;
• Encourage the listening heart;
• Proclaim well.

Select appropriate scripture passages

Selecting the appropriate scripture passages does not begin
with a Bible dictionary, or your 'favourite' scripture passage, or
what you 'feel' people need to hear from the scriptures. It is best
to begin with the practice of the church. What are the readings
of the day? What does the *Liturgical Calendar* tell us? What type
of liturgy is being planned? What is happening in this community, in the lives of the young people who will worship together? The answers will frame the foundation for decisions about
selection of scripture.

To understand the principles for the selection of scripture,
read the *Introduction to the Lectionary for Mass* and *Preparing the
Table of the Word* in this series. Here is a very brief guide.

• For eucharist on Sunday and feastdays, and on weekdays of
  Advent, Lent and Easter, the readings indicated in the
  Liturgical Calendar must be used. For other days, the first
  choice would be the readings of the day, but alternate readings may be chosen if appropriate.

• In a Roman Catholic celebration of eucharist, the greatest
  honour is given to the gospel; therefore we stand for it. The
  order of readings may include a first reading from the Old
  Testament (or in Easter Season the Acts of the Apostles), a
  psalm, a second reading from the New Testament Letters,
  Acts of the Apostles or Book of Revelation, and a proclamation of the gospel. In certain cases (*Introduction to the
  Lectionary for Mass*, 78-91), either of the first two readings
  may be omitted, but the gospel must be proclaimed.

• In morning or evening prayer, the gospel proclamation is the
  canticle sung by the whole community. The scripture proclaimed by a lector is taken from the Old Testament, or the
  New Testament Letters, Book of Acts, or Book of Revelation.
  The readings of the day may provide a suitable selection.

• In a liturgy of the word, there is value in maintaining the
  familiar order of first reading, psalm, second reading, gospel.
  Consistency in ritual helps us to participate in the common
  prayer. Singing psalms between the readings is an important
  element of the liturgy of the word, and helps the words of

faith to take root in the hearts of young believers. Sing the gospel acclamation before the gospel. Give everyone a chance to stand up and sing their praise to God who speaks to them through his Son.

- If you are preparing an extended liturgy of the word with many readings, look at the pattern in the Easter Vigil and the extended Vigil of Pentecost. The Old Testament passages that tell the story of God's salvation are intensified by the psalms that accompany them, the reading from the apostolic writings presents a clear teaching on Christian life, and the gospel proclaims the essential truth of Christ's action.

- The church has developed an order of readings that offers the richness of the word of God and provides the community with the formation and encouragement needed to live the Christian life. Following the order of readings is one aspect of being faithful to the common journey of faith shared by all in the church.

There are times, however, when the specific needs of the community indicate other scripture passages. Check out the Lectionary, which provides a valuable source of readings that fit the familiar pattern of the liturgy of the word, complement each other, offer alternative gospels, and have suitable beginnings and endings. Many options are available. If you are preparing a liturgy of the word for the afternoon of the Fourth Sunday of Easter, Year C, do not repeat the readings proclaimed at the Sunday mass. Instead, look at the Fourth Sunday of Easter, Year A or B. Or, if you are concluding a retreat based on the Beatitudes as found in Matthew's gospel, use the index in the study lectionary to find which Sunday offers that gospel, then look at the first and second readings and the psalm recommended for that Sunday and see if you can use them. They all fit together well. And to select a reading for morning prayer on a weekday in ordinary time, consider the second readings from recent Sundays, or from Sunday in another cycle.

Psalms

Morning and evening prayer, based on the singing of psalms and canticles, offers a pattern of praise and intercession that draws the entire community into a repetitive prayer rhythm. The psalms richly express every human emotion in the context of prayer. Frequent psalm-singing roots these prayers in our hearts and minds, where they echo within us long after the liturgy has been concluded, and become our words of joy, sorrow, love and wonder.

Young people who regularly pray the liturgy of the hours are formed in the language and habit of prayer. They could sing "Praise the Lord who heals the brokenhearted" (Psalm 147) in a time of grief, and, in times of doubt, "Lord you have the words of everlasting life" (Psalm 19) would reassure them. *Catholic Book of Worship III* and *Sunday Celebration of the Word and Hours* are two valuable and easily accessible resources that provide the necessities for celebrating liturgy of the hours well.

Ministers of the Word

When more than one scripture passage is proclaimed, use a different reader for each passage. A variety of voices conveys the different messages and tones of the books of the Bible. At a eucharistic celebration, properly trained lay persons are the ministers for the first and second readings, the cantor is the minister for the psalm and gospel acclamation, and the deacon (or, in his absence, a priest) is the minister of the gospel. In other liturgies, the gospel may be proclaimed by a layperson. If the scripture passage is a narrative or a dialogue, the parts may be read by different readers. However, it distorts the scripture to break a reading into parts just to provide more people with a piece to read aloud.

The most perfect piece of scripture will not nourish the community if it cannot be heard. The lector's responsibility is to give voice to the word of God with such clarity and conviction that the word is set free in the community of faith. The four cardinal rules for lectors, young or old, are unchanging: pray, prepare, practise, and proclaim. Lectors must appreciate the importance of their role, as well as the meaning and the context of the passage being proclaimed. They must pray with the passage to be filled with the spirit of the word of God. And they need to practise the reading. Those who prepare the liturgy have a responsibility to ensure readers are competent and well prepared, and to correct those faults which interfere with the hearing of God's word. It is inexcusable to continue to use lectors who proclaim carelessly or inadequately. The community is entitled to hear the Word. "The readings lay the table of God's Word for the faithful and open up the riches of the Bible to them" (*GIRM*, 34).

Use the very best materials available. How many times in youth group have the scripture been proclaimed from a shabby, dog-eared copy of the *Good News Bible* which is put on the floor after the proclamation? The way we treat the scriptures expresses our respect for the word of God. Use the Lectionary, or a Bible in a suitable translation—in good condition. Treat the book with respect. Never put it on the floor. Place it on the ambo, or on a suitably prepared table.

Proclaim from the ambo which has been located in a place where the lector can be seen and heard by the entire assembly. If the ambo is not available, or is not suitable for the needs of the group, prepare an appropriate table for the book.

If the space requires it, use the necessary sound equipment to allow the readings to be heard. Before the celebration begins, give the readers adequate time to practise with the microphones and ensure the sound system functions properly. Correct any problems.

Encourage listening hearts. Be a good model, offer educational opportunities, lobby for good homilists, and live in the generous way which testifies to the power of God's word. Avoid fundamentalism, but offer guidance from the scriptures. Introduce young people to the figures of the Bible, both weak and strong, serious and comic. Work with lectors. Proclaim well. Incorporate reflection on the scriptures into liturgy planning. Select appropriate scripture passages for the community. Encourage prayer with scripture. Live in the scriptures and the liturgical year.

Reflecting on the Scriptures

The reflection following the proclamation of scripture may take many forms. The presider may preach, or may designate another person to preach (*Directory for Masses with Children*, 24). There may be a dramatization, or a sung meditation. Whatever form the reflection after the scripture takes, its goal is the same. The reflection must point to and make clear to all the point of intersection between the truths of God proclaimed in the scripture, the tradition and faith of the church, and the lives of those who hear the word. That is the preacher's responsibility, and it is not to be taken lightly. Reflections which do not fulfill it have failed to meet this responsibility—and the chance to break open God's word within the community of faith that day may be lost.

Anyone who has ever prayed with the scriptures knows that the gospels continually yield new treasures. It is the homilist's responsibility to foster the treasure hunt. Preaching is not a catechetical session. The temptation to teach young people everything they need to know in one large lesson, just because they are captive in front of you, must be avoided as the falsehood it is. Those preparing the celebration must let the homilist know enough about the lives of those participating to be able to point to where the word of God is bearing fruit.

Dance and Drama

In liturgies celebrated with young people, both drama and dance can serve to draw the assembly more directly into the liturgical act. Dance and/or choreographed gesture may occur in one of two ways. Some individuals who move with grace and beauty may lead the procession, dress the table and carry incense; alternatively, the entire community may join in some ritual gesture, such as waving palms while singing Hosannas on Palm Sunday, or in some movements that express a prayer, for instance, accompanying the intercessory prayer with a ges-

ture that matches the music. Dance and gesture are always servants of the liturgy, not interruptions or entertainment. If the community is to join in a common gesture, the presider is responsible to ensure individuals have the information necessary to participate and can do so within the space and setting. In planning liturgies with young people, be aware that they can undergo periods of extreme self-consciousness about their bodies and may resist joining in a gesture they have previously enjoyed.

On occasion, reflection on the scriptures may take the form of a drama. It must be carefully prepared, not just a spontaneous 'ad-lib' that could trivialize the liturgical event. It must relate directly to the scriptures which have been proclaimed. Avoid putting on a skit from a canned script that makes some point about Christian morality, but fails to connect to the liturgy or the scripture. Keep the use of costumes and props to a minimum. Don't reduce the assembly to an audience watching a show.

Another alternative is to develop drama after the liturgy, as a reflection on the worship experience. It can effectively explore the various layers of the meaning of the experience.

Music

Young people value music as an expression of themselves. It speaks of their daily reality, their hopes and dreams, their fears and disappointments, and their ordinary experiences of life in a way that plain words cannot. Today's young people rate music as second in importance only to their friends (*Teen Trends: A Nation in Motion*. Reginald W. Bibby and Donald C. Posterski [Toronto: Stoddard Publishing, 1992], 20). For their celebrations of faith life, therefore, the selection of music is of great importance. *Music in Catholic Worship* states its value this way: "Among the many signs and symbols used by the church to celebrate its faith, music is of preeminent importance. Music should assist the assembled believers to express and share the gift of faith that is within them, and to nourish and strengthen their interior commitment of faith" (23). That is exactly what we hope happens in our liturgy.

The standard of excellence and authenticity demanded by our participation in Christ's act of thanksgiving to the Father is the measure of the music with which the community joins in praise. While many types of music and a variety of instruments may serve the liturgy, all is to be done with care and integrity. Music serves the prayer of the church, and those who offer that prayer. Music must be chosen, therefore, to express the scriptural images and prayer words of the liturgy, and to provide a bridge whereby young people may enter the worship experience. Instrumental accompaniment, hand clapping, and other gestures will contribute to raising the energy level and will heighten the experience of participation.

Singing along to taped music reduces the worshippers to echo status or a karaoke act; therefore it is inappropriate to liturgy. If the particular song is suitable to the liturgy, let the community learn the song and sing it with or without musical accompaniment. If the music cannot be sung or played by members of this specific assembly, it does not meet the liturgical and pastoral criteria for music at this liturgy. Taped music is appropriate to a quiet time of reflection and individual prayer, and may serve a group in a retreat setting, or in preparation for liturgy, but has no place in the liturgical event.

Music is the servant of the community's worship. Musical, liturgical, and pastoral judgments determine the selection of music for liturgy. For more on these judgments, see *Preparing Music for Celebration* in this series.

To choose music and appropriate instrumentation, select the place and duration of each song, identify and deploy skilled musicians, and foster the assembly's participation requires good musical judgment. The music itself must be of good quality. Poor rhythms, trite melodies, boring repetitions, pretentious or overblown instrumentation indicate that the material is unsuitable for liturgical use.

The liturgical judgment is based on the needs of the liturgy itself. The very specific role music plays in the liturgy determines the type of music chosen and the manner in which it is sung. The lyrics need to make the connection with the reality of the church, reflecting scriptural images, prayer language and the human experience. The music itself must serve the action of the liturgy. A hymn for the entrance procession requires the kind of pace that expresses a community moving forward to the kingdom, not a leisurely skate on the canal. The communion song is intended to bind all in a shared experience of feasting at the Lord's banquet table, not encourage individuals to private meditation. Certain prayers, such as the acclamations in the eucharistic prayer (the Holy, Memorial Acclamation, and Great Amen) form a unity that is enhanced by common musical elements. Singing four hymns while speaking these acclamations, or playing an elaborate musical piece to accompany the presentation of the gifts and preparation of the altar while providing only a brief communion hymn distorts the order of importance of the liturgical elements and disturbs the balance of the celebration.

The pastoral judgment is most often the deciding factor, for it is based on the specific needs of the actual worshipping community. The age and the level of faith as well as the cultural and social environment of worshippers must be considered in all factors of liturgy preparation, including the selection of music. When you consider using contemporary music at liturgy, look out for the individualism which is so much a part of contemporary culture. It is inappropriate to sing lyrics that speak only of 'me' and my needs, that describe God as some kind of 'magic fixer' or 'super spy.' Pastoral judgment asks such questions as: "Which musical selections will best serve the unity of this particular group?" "Which processional hymn will best express the faith experience of these worshippers?" "Which mass setting do they know?" "Which music will invite worshippers into the common life of the church?"

In selecting music for celebrations with youth it is helpful if the choices bear some relationship to the kind of music experienced at the parish Sunday assembly. This may mean the young musicians share their musical skills on Sunday morning, or that some pieces of music are used both for the parish mass on

Sunday and the school celebration on Wednesday, or that the lyrics are similar. It should mean that the same principles of music selection and use are applied in both liturgies. If the young person joyfully sings the refrain while coming forward in the communion procession at the mass with youth, but the parish tradition is a solo meditation offered by a whispery soprano, there is fertile soil for discomfort and discouragement. It is not helpful to carry out the "battle of the bands" in the liturgical life of our young people and in our parishes. Since music imprints young people so effectively, a continuing and glaring difference between the two celebrations can make it more difficult for young people to enter any worship experience.

Remember that young people play an enormous variety of instruments. Be prepared, both in the parish, and in other settings, to call on this kind of musical talent to serve the liturgy. Many pieces of contemporary liturgical music are scored for a variety of instruments. While you may not be able to (nor should you necessarily) use all the instruments in any one celebration, don't hesitate to try out innovative combinations in different celebrations.

Tools for Participation

Participation aids

Participation aids are an expression of hospitality, enabling people to take part more actively in the liturgy, and reducing the number of times a leader of song or presider must interrupt the community's prayer to give instructions. They must always provide correct information in an accessible manner that reflects the importance of the act of worship.

The simplest and most familiar aid is the hymn number board, which delivers basic information in a direct manner. It must be clearly visible to all in the assembly, and in good condition. Nothing shabby at liturgy!

Printed programs come in two basic formats, one for use with a hymnal and one that provides all the text necessary for participation. Creating a printed program that assists participation is a worthy act of liturgical preparation. Use your best materials and your finest talents to create a program which invites people to share in this important event. When working with young people, it helps if you simply acknowledge and accept that there are certain times when some young people can and will make airplanes or missiles out of almost anything.

The colour of the paper may reflect the liturgical season or the nature of the event, but the shade and texture must allow the type to stand out clearly. Some shades are too bright or too dark for clarity, and make reading almost impossible.

The typeface also must serve the demand for legibility. The best choices are clear and crisp, with a minimum of flourishes.

A program the size of a bookmark, printed on card stock, which situates the liturgy and provides necessary participation information is very helpful, if you are using a hymnal. Welcome worshippers with the bookmark already inserted in the hymnal at the opening hymn.

When you do not have hymnals available for the whole community, it is helpful to provide a printed program which satisfies these essential requirements:

- Print all of and only those words that people need to participate.
- Do not print all the words spoken by the presider or the reader or the cantor. Listening, not reading, is essential to participation.
- Print posture instructions in place. Make them distinct from the prayer texts by the typeface and location.
- Print words for all music sung by the entire community. Be scrupulous about copyright—you are modelling an act of justice.
- Prepare the program carefully as another expression of the essential importance of liturgy. Typos, crooked layouts, ripped paper, smudges all convey carelessness and lack of respect.
- Do not put any extra reading material in the program. This is not the place for wise sayings, jokes, or cartoons.

Distributing the programs as people arrive is a practical act of hospitality and welcome that ensures every person present at the liturgy has a copy of the program.

Be ecologically responsible with printed material. Remove all paper from the worship space when the liturgy is finished, and recycle as fully as possible.

In Summary

1. Young people, fully initiated and properly prepared, share in the community's responsibility to assume the liturgical roles needed for good celebration.

2. The order of readings provided by the Lectionary nourishes people well; the psalms are powerful prayers that can sustain young people in their times of crisis and growth.

3. Ministers of the word must prepare carefully.

4. The preacher is the guide who points to God's action in life, liturgy and scripture.

5. Well-prepared and appropriate dance and drama can draw young people more deeply into the liturgy.

Discussion Questions

1. How is the assembly the first minister of prayer?

2. How can young people reflect on the scriptures?

3. Why do the scripture selections affect the choice of music?

44

Formed in Praise for Service

Young people have a profound capacity for God. They are living a time of rich growth, every day becoming more deeply aware of the ambiguities and perplexities of life. These are the days when they first become cynics, and first fall in love. These are the years when they begin to discover the mysteries of the scientific universe, and at the same time give themselves over to absolute silliness that has no meaning for anyone over a certain age. These are the moments when they form true friendships with adults, and discover the failures of their own parents. And in all of this discovery and revelation, they come to know loneliness and loss, hope and joy. They are ready to come to know and love God in a totally new way, different from their former trusting childhood self, and also different from their future, integrated adult self. The young person is ready to come to know and love the divine in questions and rushes of rich emotion, in anger and absolute delight, in intellect, feeling and action.

All of this knowing and loving can be nurtured, supported and enriched in good liturgy. As the young people of a parish participate in liturgies that speak to their own realities, their sense of belonging to this larger community of faith, and to this God who calls them to the new life of grace is reinforced.

But this is not enough. Our preparation of and participation in liturgy is not "art for art's sake," nor is it an exercise in exactness and relationality, or in making people feel good. Liturgy is our communal act of worship of the God of the beatitudes, the God who heals the brokenhearted, feeds the hungry and clothes the naked, the God who comes to bring salvation to the nations. This common action must send us out into the world to be the body of Christ for those who may never come inside a church. The young people who participate in liturgy go to places their parents and pastors and youth ministers cannot go, and they must go from this liturgy to bring the Lord to those places.

All the guidelines, all the books, all the preparation and training in the whole world serve a single purpose: to form a community of believers who praise God. Participating in this praise forms worshippers into the body of Christ, and they go forth into the world to bring the good news of a loving God to all they meet. Faith becomes a verb at worship, propelling all into the world to bear witness to the One who has loved us. And that work in the world sends us back to worship, back to offer thanks and praise to God, back to be supported and sustained in our lives of discipleship, in our best times, our worst times, and those ordinary days in between.

BIBLIOGRAPHY

Recommended Reading

Ritual books

The *Liturgical Calendar* is an annual publication of the Canadian Conference of Catholic Bishops. It begins with the First Sunday of Advent and provides essential information for every day of the church year. The liturgical season, the feast day, the readings, the colour of the vestments, the sacramentary selections, all this and more is listed in the *Calendar*, which is usually found in an easily accessible spot in the sacristy.

The *Lectionary* makes the scriptures available in the language and form the church has determined to be most suitable to the liturgical celebration. The study edition of the Lectionary, a soft-covered, more compact book, has a pronunciation guide which is really helpful for readers to practise the readings, and a table of readings which indicates the location of any scripture passage.

The *Sacramentary* is the large book from which the priest proclaims the prayers at mass. It contains all the ritual prayers for the celebration of eucharist and other important events of the church as well as prayers for many occasions, model intercessions, greetings and solemn blessings. Liturgical instructions are also printed throughout the *Sacramentary*.

Catholic Book of Worship III provides a rich variety of suitable music for all liturgies and a number of indices that guide liturgy preparation and music selection, simplifying the choice of suitable music for any liturgical event. Includes an outline of basic liturgies with musical recommendations in place. Can pray morning and evening prayer from it.

Sunday Celebration of the Word and the Hours provides alternatives to the Sunday eucharist for communities without a priest. Provides good models for a liturgy of the word, and morning and evening prayer. This new ritual book may come to serve a broader purpose than its title indicates.

Books

Bibby, Reginald W. and Posterski, Donald C. *Teen Trends: A Nation in Motion*. Toronto: Stoddart, 1992. A valuable sociological study of Canadian youth and culture, based on nationwide surveys. Excellent section on the role of religion.

Dues, Greg. *Why Go to Mass*. Mystic, CT: Twenty-Third Publications, 1994. Very useful material for working with teens in discussing participation in eucharist.

Foot, David K. and Stoffman, Daniel. *Boom, Bust and Echo*. Toronto: Macfarlane, Walter & Ross, 1996. A fascinating study of current and future Canadian economic, social and cultural demographic realities.

Gura, Carol. *Ministering to Young Adults*. Winona, MN: Saint Mary's Press, 1987. A good example of the resource materials available for ministry with youth and young adults.

Harris, Maria. *Portrait of Youth Ministry*. New York: Paulist Press, 1981. Although dated in reference to music, etc., this basic book lays good foundation for youth ministry.

Roberto, John. *Liturgy & Worship*. New Rochelle, NY: Don Bosco Multimedia, 1994. One of the *Guides to Youth Ministry Series*.

Warren, Michael. *Readings and Resources in Youth Ministry*. Winona, MN: Saint Mary's Press, 1987. A broad selection of helpful readings in youth ministry.

Periodicals

Caravan, A Resource for Adult Religious Educators. Ottawa: CCCB. A valuable Canadian resource that provides helpful, current, usable material in many areas of faith life.

Celebrate! Ottawa: Novalis. Published six times yearly, *Celebrate!* provides solid up-to-date resources on a wide range of pastoral liturgical issues and background for working with the Sunday readings.

Group. Loveland, CO: Group Pub Co. Interesting, current articles on Christian youth, family life, society, music, etc.

National Bulletin on Liturgy. Ottawa: CCCB. Published by the National Liturgy Office of the Canadian Conference of Catholic Bishops. Solid, scholarly articles on various liturgical issues.

Youth Update. Cincinnati, OH: St. Anthony Messenger Press. A truly helpful series that addresses issues of interest to young people and those working with them. Good language and simple explanations facilitate informed discussion of important issues.

Youthworker Update. Birmingham, ALA: CCM Communications. An American publication that gathers articles and information about the culture and concerns of young people.